SCOTTISH CURIOSITIES

Discover the Legends and Mysteries of Scotland

Lincoln Alencar

"Scottish Curiosities"

© 2024 by Lincoln Alencar. All rights reserved.

Edited by Cameron Burns

No part of this publication may be reproduced, distributed, or transmitted in any form or by any means, including photocopying, recording, or other electronic or mechanical methods, without the prior written permission of the publisher, except in the case of brief quotations embodied in critical reviews and certain other non-commercial uses permitted by copyright law.

ISBN: 9798322372981

Visit our "Scotland Live" website

<u>https://scotlandlive.org</u>

and follow our Instagram page

https://instagram.com/scotland.live

CONTENTS

Dedication	9
Introduction	11
A Gift for You	14
Part I: A Land of History and Mystery	18
Part II. Natural Wonders	58
Part III: Manmade Wonders	72
Part IV: Culture, Traditions, and Innovations	93
Part V: Random Curiosities	111
Conclusion	137
Appendix	139

DEDICATION

To the indomitable spirit of Scotland and its guardians through the ages; those who have shaped its land, culture, and stories with their bravery and passion.

And to the readers and travelers, whose thirst for knowledge and adventure takes us beyond the pages of this book, in search of the mysteries and wonders that await in every corner of the world. May this book be a window to the soul of Scotland, inviting all to explore, dream, and discover.

INTRODUCTION

Welcome to a land of shadow and light, where history intertwines with myth, and reality dances with legends. Scotland, with its misty valleys, ancient castles, and landscapes that defy imagination, is more than a country in the northern part of Great Britain: it is a realm of mysteries and wonders, where every stone and river has a story to tell. This book is an invitation to cross the veil of the ordinary and explore the deepest secrets and most fascinating curiosities that this ancient land has to offer.

From the hidden depths of Gilmerton Cove, to the mysterious carvings left by the Picts, Scotland is a treasure trove of stories waiting to be discovered. Through each chapter of this book we will uncover the veils shrouding some of the most intriguing enigmas of the Scottish nation, navigating through tales of cannibal clans hidden in coastal caves and secret gardens rivalling the wonders of Versailles.

Prepare yourself for a journey that will challenge your perception of what is possible, diving into the enigmatic waters of Loch Ness in search of Nessie, and venturing off the beaten path to the Poison Gardens of Alnwick, where the deadly beauty of plants unveils stories of both healing and destruction. The Underground City of Edinburgh awaits us with its mysteries hidden beneath the bustling streets, while the Lewis Chessmen offer an enigmatic glimpse into Scotland's Viking connections and their enduring influence.

Each story and secret revealed in these pages is a testament to Scotland's rich cultural tapestry, a land where the past and present coexist in a vibrant and tangible manner. From the brutality of ancient clans to the innovations that shaped the modern world, from the serenity of secret gardens to the ferocity of battles echoing through the centuries, this book seeks not just to inform, but also to inspire and ignite curiosity.

With every page turned, you will be invited to look beyond the clichés, to delve deeper into the essence of Scotland—a nation forged in fire and water, tradition, and rebellion. This is not just a collection of curiosities: it is a celebration of the indomitable Scottish spirit, the breathtaking beauty of its lands, and the unfathomable depth of its stories.

Join us on this extraordinary journey, as we unravel the secrets and wonders of Scotland: a land where each discovery is an invitation to dream bigger, explore deeper, and marvel at the incredible tapestry of life.

A GIFT FOR YOU

Dear reader,

As a token of our appreciation for embarking on this journey with us, we are delighted to offer you a gift for you. We believe that curiosity is the key that unlocks all doors to knowledge and adventure. And, to continue fuelling that curiosity about Scotland and its wonders we would like to invite you to be part of a very special group.

You now have access to our exclusive group content on Instagram! That's right, a digital passport that allows you to dive even deeper into the curiosities, mysteries, and beauties of Scotland. There, we'll share exclusive content, untold stories, stunning images, and much more, all thoughtfully crafted just for you, our curious and adventurous reader.

To access this unique content, simply use your phone to scan the QR Code below. It will redirect you directly to our exclusive group on Instagram, where the magic of Scotland continues to unfold in colours, words, and sounds.

Oidhche air Beinn
(A Night on the Mountain)

Oidhche air Beinn
(A Night on the Mountain)

Ann an sàmhchair na h-oidhche,
(In the quiet of the night,)

Fo sgàil a' bheinn, tha mi nam shuidhe;
(Under the mountain's shadow, I sit;)

Rionnagan a' deàrrsadh gu binn,
(Stars twinkle sweetly,)

A' moladh dìomhaireachd na cruinne.
(Praising the universe's mystery.)

Gaoth a' seideadh tro na coilltean,
(Wind blows through the woods,)

A' glaodhaich le fuaim na h-uisge;
(Calling with the sound of water;)

Ceòl na h-Alba, domhain is fìor,
(Scotland's music, deep and true,)

A' toirt solas dhan anam ciùin.
(Brings light to the peaceful soul.)

Seasamh làidir, a' coimhead thairis,
(Standing strong, looking over,)

Air lochan ciùin is beanntan àrda;
(Over calm lochs and high mountains;)

An dùthaich seo, cridhe mo chridhe,
(This land, the heart of my heart,)

Alba, 's tu mo ghaol, gun chrìoch.
(Scotland, you are my love, endless.)

PART I

A LAND OF HISTORY AND MYSTERY

THE SECRET TUNNEL OF GILMERTON COVE

Beneath the bustling streets on the outskirts of Edinburgh lies an enigma buried in the underground of Gilmerton Cove. This labyrinth of hand-carved tunnels and chambers cut into the sandstone tells a story not found in conventional history books. The origin and purpose of these tunnels remain a mystery, fuelling speculation and urban legends.

Officially discovered in the 18th century, some believe these tunnels were created as a refuge for members of secret religious cults, while others argue they served as hideouts for smugglers. There are also theories suggesting Gilmerton Cove was a meeting point for secret societies, such as the Freemasons. The undeniable skill and effort required to carve such a network of chambers in solid rock point to a significant motivation behind their creation.

Visiting Gilmerton Cove is a unique experience, inviting visitors to literally dive deep into Scottish history. The subterranean chambers, with their peculiar features like benches carved into the rock, tables, and even a well, spark the imagination about their uses. This mysterious site offers an intriguing window into an undocumented past, leaving more questions than answers about the lives and intentions of its creators.

THE UNKNOWN PICTISH SYMBOLS

The Picts, one of Scotland's most mysterious societies, left behind an enigmatic legacy: stones carved with symbols whose meanings have been lost to time. These stones found throughout Scotland and feature a variety of designs including spirals, stylised animals, and abstract geometric shapes. The function and meaning of these symbols have been the subject of debate among historians and archaeologists for centuries.

Some scholars suggest that the symbols had a religious or spiritual purpose, possibly related to nature worship rituals or marking sacred territories. Other theories propose that they served as a form of communication or record-keeping, perhaps even a symbolic writing system.

The fascinating complexity and consistency of these symbols across different locations and periods suggest a shared meaning among the Picts.

Despite advancements in archaeology and symbol analysis, the true purpose of these stones and the meanings of the Pictish symbols remain one of Scotland's great ancient mysteries. This enigma not only fuels fascination with the Pictish culture but also highlights the complexity of ancient societies and humanity's ongoing quest to understand its past.

THE LEGEND OF SAWNEY BEAN

The legend of Sawney Bean is one of the most grim and disturbing tales of Scotland, telling the story of a man and his family who were said to have lived off cannibalism in the coastal caves during the 16th century. According to legend, Alexander "Sawney" Bean led his extensive family, consisting of his wife, children, and grandchildren — many of whom were the product of incest

— in a series of deadly ambushes against unsuspecting travellers, whose bodies were taken to the cave to be eaten.

The myth states that the Bean family remained undetected for years, thanks to the seclusion of their cave and the cunning methods they used to capture their victims. Eventually, after a failed attack that resulted in the escape of a victim, the royal authorities were notified, leading to a massive search that culminated in the discovery of the horror-filled cave inhabited by the Bean family. The legend ends with the capture and summary execution of all family members, without trial.

While the true existence of Sawney Bean is subject to debate, with some historians questioning the veracity of the story and suggesting it may have been anti-Scottish propaganda or an urban legend of the time, the legend of Sawney Bean captures the imagination and highlights the dark fascination that tales of horror and cannibalism have on us.

THE ENIGMATIC CASE OF THE GREAT MULL AIR MYSTERY

The enigmatic case of The Great Mull Air Mystery centres on the vanishing of Norman Peter Gibbs, an adept aviator boasting over 2,000 flight hours. On the eve of December 24, 1975, Gibbs embarked on an impromptu solo flight at night from the Glenforsa Airfield, situated on the Isle of Mull, Scotland, piloting a Cessna

F150H. Despite his proficient aviation skills, Gibbs and his aircraft mysteriously failed to return, igniting one of the most perplexing unsolved mysteries in Scottish aviation history.

The narrative unfolds with Gibbs and his partner enjoying their evening at the Glenforsa Hotel, their accommodation of choice. Following their meal, and despite the discouragement from hotel personnel and the unfavorable weather conditions, Gibbs was determined to take to the skies. He ingeniously employed flashlights, handled by his partner at the airstrip's end, as improvised landing illumination. Eyewitnesses recounted Gibbs' departure into the pitch-black night, marking the last occasion he was observed alive.

In a startling discovery made four months afterward, in April 1976, Gibbs' body was located by a shepherd on a hillside, not far from the airstrip, remarkably without any significant injuries. This area had undergone previous searches, and the sudden discovery of his body in such a frequented zone provoked widespread speculation. Exposure was declared the cause of death, yet how Gibbs found himself on that hillside remains an enigma. Despite numerous hypotheses and thorough searches, Gibbs'

Cessna has yet to be officially located, leaving the details surrounding his final flight shrouded in mystery.

Years later, speculative findings concerning the aircraft emerged, notably a 1986 report from a clam diver who allegedly encountered a small aircraft submerged near Oban, and a 2004 sighting by minesweepers who identified wreckage resembling Gibbs' Cessna. Nonetheless, these leads have yet to definitively unravel the enigma. The case persists, open and subject to a variety of theories concerning Gibbs' motives and the sequence of events that culminated in his mysterious demise.

CLAN HISTORY

Clan history is a fundamental element of Scotland's cultural heritage. Clans, originating in the Highlands, were family groups led by a chief, each with their own tartan, coat of arms and war cry. This tradition reflects the rich tapestry of loyalties and identities within Scottish society.

Each clan has a unique history, often marked by heroic battles, political alliances and the fight for survival in adverse landscapes. Clans have played a crucial role in Scotland's historical events, shaping the country's identity over the centuries.

Today, clans continue to be a source of pride for many Scots, with Highland festivals and games celebrating this ancient heritage. Tartans, in particular, have become a globally recognised symbol of Scotland and its vibrant history.

THE MASSACRE OF THE ISLE OF EIGG

Another dark tale in Scottish history is the Massacre of the Isle of Eigg. In 1577, a conflict between the MacDonald clan of Eigg and visiting members of the MacLeod clan from Skye triggered a chain of events that would culminate in tragedy. Following a dispute that led to the humiliation of the MacLeods, they returned in greater numbers to seek revenge. The MacDonalds, anticipating retaliation, hid in a cave now known as Massacre Cave.

The MacLeods, unable to find the MacDonalds, were preparing to leave the island when they spotted a single lookout. Following him to the cave, they decided to set a large fire at the entrance, suffocating to death all those hidden inside. More than 400 members of the MacDonald clan died, marking one of the most brutal episodes of clan disputes in Scotland.

This massacre is not only a testament to the bloody disputes that occurred between Scottish clans but also reflects the brutality of life in medieval Scotland and the long shadow such events cast over local history. The massacre cave, now a grim tourist spot, serves as a somber reminder of this tragedy and the complex web of alliances and enmities that characterised Scottish society at the time.

These narratives weave together history and myth, offering a glimpse into the darker layers of Scottish culture, where the beauty of the landscapes contrasts with tales of horror that resonate through the centuries.

EDINBURGH'S DARK TALE: THE SECRET TUNNELS AND THE MACABRE BUSINESS OF BURKE AND HARE

Edinburgh, a city rich in history and mystery, is home to one of the darkest tales of the 19th century, intricately tied to its culture, traditions, and innovations: the murders committed by William Burke and William Hare. This story not only highlights the macabre nature of some chapters of the city's past but also reveals the existence of secret tunnels beneath the streets of Edinburgh, which played a crucial role during this grim period.

Burke and Hare became infamous for murdering 16 people over the course of a year, from 1827 to 1828. The motive behind these heinous acts was to sell the victims' bodies to the Edinburgh Medical School, where they would be used for anatomical studies. At that time, there was a growing demand for cadavers for medical research, but the legal supply through executions was insufficient to meet the needs of medical students and researchers.

Legend has it that Burke and Hare used Edinburgh's secret tunnels to transport the bodies of their victims to the medical school, thus avoiding detection. These tunnels, part of an underground complex known as "Edinburgh's Underground City," were originally intended for storage and the passage of goods but ended up facilitating one of the city's most notorious episodes.

After the capture of Burke and Hare, public outrage led to changes in the laws regarding body dissection, allowing unclaimed bodies to be used for medical studies, which eliminated the need for the illegal trade in bodies. Burke was sentenced to death and hanged, and his body was, ironically, dissected at the Edinburgh Medical School. Hare was granted immunity in exchange for his testimony against Burke and vanished into obscurity.

The story of Burke and Hare remains as a somber reminder of Edinburgh's macabre past and the existence of the city's mysterious underground tunnels, which, according to reports, are still there, winding beneath the historic streets, carrying with them the secrets of a bygone era. This narrative is a chilling chapter in the broader context of Edinburgh's culture, traditions, and the dark side of its innovations.

THE GREYFRIARS KIRKYARD IN EDINBURGH

The Greyfriars Kirkyard in Edinburgh is not only famous for its historical significance and as the final resting place of notable Scottish figures, but it's also infamous for being home to one of the most well-documented paranormal phenomena in the world: the

Mackenzie Poltergeist. This ghostly presence is associated with the tomb of Sir George Mackenzie, a 17th-century lawyer who played a key role in the persecution of the Covenanters, a religious group that opposed King Charles II's attempts to impose Anglicanism in Scotland.

Background on Sir George Mackenzie

Sir George Mackenzie, known as "Bluidy Mackenzie," was the Lord Advocate during the reign of Charles II and was responsible for the imprisonment, torture, and execution of numerous Covenanters. His actions earned him a fearsome reputation, both in life and death. Mackenzie was buried in the Black Mausoleum within Greyfriars Kirkyard after his death in 1691.

The Mackenzie Poltergeist

The phenomena associated with the Mackenzie Poltergeist began to be widely reported in the late 20th century after a homeless person reportedly broke into Mackenzie's tomb. Since then, visitors and ghost tour participants have reported a wide range of unsettling experiences near the Black Mausoleum and in other parts of the kirkyard. These experiences include sudden drops in temperature, unexplained bruises, scratches, and even feelings of being pushed or choked by an invisible force.

Investigating the Phenomena

The Mackenzie Poltergeist has attracted the attention of paranormal investigators from around the globe. Numerous attempts have been made to document and understand the activity, with varying degrees of skepticism. While some investigators attribute the phenomena to psychological factors or suggestible participants, others believe the activity to be genuine evidence of paranormal occurrences.

Greyfriars Kirkyard Today

Today, Greyfriars Kirkyard remains a popular destination for both history enthusiasts and those interested in the paranormal. The stories of the Mackenzie Poltergeist have become an integral part of Edinburgh's ghost tours, attracting visitors keen to experience the eerie atmosphere of the kirkyard for themselves. Despite the fear and intrigue surrounding the Black Mausoleum, Greyfriars Kirkyard is also appreciated for its historical significance, beauty, and tranquility, standing as a testament to Edinburgh's rich and complex history.

ISOBEL GOWDIE: THE QUEEN OF SCOTTISH WITCHES

One of the most intriguing mysteries that permeate Scottish history involves Isobel Gowdie, the woman who became synonymous with witchcraft and sorcery in 17th-century Scotland. The story of Isobel Gowdie is fascinating not just for the extraordinary details of her confessions but also for the cultural and social context in which they occurred, illustrating Scotland's enduring fascination with magic and the supernatural.

Isobel Gowdie, a woman from the village of Auldearn, near Nairn, made waves through history with her detailed confessions about witchcraft, professed without evidence of torture, which was unusual for the time. During the height of the witch hunts in Europe in the 17th century, Gowdie voluntarily confessed to being part of a coven of witches that, according to her, could transform into animals, fly on broomsticks, and cast spells and curses against local inhabitants.

The Confessions and Spells

Isobel's confessions, recorded in 1662, contain detailed descriptions of encounters with the Devil, spells cast upon her neighbours, and nocturnal meetings with other witches. She described transforming into a crow or hare to escape detection and detailed the enchantments used to control the elements and influence community events. Isobel also spoke of journeys to the "Fairy Realm," a recurring theme in Celtic folklore, where she and her fellow witches met with faerie beings.

The story of Isobel Gowdie remains one of the most detailed and vivid accounts of Scottish witchcraft, significantly contributing to our understanding of witchcraft practices in Scotland and the supernatural beliefs of the time. Her confessions offer a rare glimpse into the magical traditions that were an integral part of Scottish folklore, as well as the harsh realities faced by those accused of witchcraft.

The contemporary fascination with Isobel Gowdie reflects the ongoing interest in magic, witchcraft, and the power of the feminine in the context of the supernatural. Isobel's story transcends time, remaining a powerful testament to the beliefs and fears that shaped Scottish society and continues to inspire works of literature, music, and art, serving as a reminder of the complex relationship between magic, religion, and power in Scottish history.

Isobel Gowdie's story is an enthralling mystery that highlights the rich tapestry of myths, magic, and witchcraft in Scotland, a country where the veil between the natural and supernatural worlds has always been considered particularly thin.

THE UNDERGROUND CITY OF EDINBURGH

Beneath the cobblestone streets of Edinburgh lies a forgotten world, a labyrinth of rooms and corridors known as the Underground City. Originating in the 17th and 18th centuries, these subterranean chambers were built to accommodate the city's rapid population growth and, over time, became a refuge for the poorest in society. However, the history of the Underground City is marked by much more than just misery and despair: it is permeated by reports of paranormal activities that persist to this day.

Visitors and tour guides frequently report encounters with the supernatural in the dark passageways beneath Edinburgh. The most famous of these apparitions is a young girl, lost in the shadows, seeking someone to help her find peace. Unexplained sounds, such as footsteps and whispers, echo off the walls, while sensations of invisible touches and sudden drops in temperature are common experiences among those brave enough to explore its depths.

The Underground City offers a window into Edinburgh's tumultuous past, a time when disease, poverty, and overcrowding were part of everyday life. Today, these chambers serve as a grim reminder of the city's history, drawing curious people and ghost hunters from around the world, eager to explore its mysteries.

THE ENIGMA OF THE LEWIS CHESSMEN

The Lewis Chessmen, a set of medieval chess pieces discovered on the Isle of Lewis in 1831, remain one of Scotland's most enigmatic archaeological treasures. Made from walrus ivory and whale teeth, these pieces exhibit a level of craftsmanship and detail that suggests a noble origin, possibly linked to Norway, where similar pieces were produced during the 12th century.

The discovery of the pieces, buried in a stone chest, raised numerous questions about how they arrived on the remote Scottish island and who might have buried them. Some historians suggest the pieces were lost by Nordic traders, while others believe they were a hidden treasure, perhaps belonging to a noble on the run.

The Lewis Chessmen are not just objects of admiration for their beauty and mystery; they also offer a fascinating glimpse into the medieval world, a time when chess games were a popular form of entertainment among the elite. Today, the pieces are considered national icons of Scotland, displayed in museums and admired for their enigmatic history and their connection to the country's Viking past.

EDINBURGH CASTLE: TALES FROM BEYOND THE GRAVE

Edinburgh Castle is not just one of Scotland's most significant historical landmarks: it's also one of its most haunted. Built on an ancient volcanic rock, the castle has been a site of great historical and strategic significance since the 12th century. With such a long and often bloody history, it's no surprise that it is home to numerous ghosts.

Among the many tales, one of the most disturbing is that of the headless drummer boy, whose ghost is said to appear when the castle is about to be attacked. Another frequent apparition is that of a prisoner from the Seven Years' War, seen in the dungeons, still wearing his uniform, marked by the battles he fought.

Visitors to the castle report supernatural experiences, from the sensation of being watched to direct encounters with apparitions. The presence of these spirits, whether real or the product of collective imagination, adds an extra layer of mystery to this ancient stronghold, enriching the tapestry of Scotland's cultural heritage with stories that challenge explanation.

THE MYSTERY OF "GLASGOW'S TIME CAPSULE"

The mystery of "Glasgow's Time Capsule" refers to a series of time capsules buried at secret locations throughout the city of Glasgow. These capsules, many of which have yet to be discovered, represent historical puzzles that captivate both locals and historians alike. The practice of burying time capsules is a way to preserve history and culture for future generations, containing items or documents that reflect the era in which they were sealed.

While some of these capsules have been unearthed and opened, revealing slices of everyday life, significant events, and memories from the time they were buried, many others remain hidden. The exact content and location of these undiscovered time capsules are unknown, fuelling speculation and curiosity about what they might contain. There could be capsules under historic buildings, parks, or other emblematic sites of the city, waiting for the right time to be revealed.

This mystery adds an intriguing layer to Glasgow's rich historical tapestry, inviting city dwellers and visitors alike to wonder about the stories and secrets waiting to be uncovered. Glasgow's time capsules are a fascinating reminder that, amidst the fast pace of modern life, there are hidden treasures that connect the present to the past in mysterious and wonderful ways.

THE STONE OF DESTINY

The Stone of Destiny, also known as the Stone of Scone, is an artefact steeped in history and mysticism, central to Scotland's national identity. This ancient stone, used in the coronations of Scottish and later British monarchs, is surrounded by legends and stories that span centuries.

Origins and History

The Stone of Destiny is believed to have originally been used as a ceremonial object by the ancient druids and Scottish kings. According to legend, the stone was brought to Scotland from Ireland (and before that, possibly from Palestine) by Fergus Mór mac Eirc, one of Scotland's first kings, becoming a symbol of the Scottish right to the throne.

Ceremonial Importance

Historically kept at Scone Abbey, near Perth, the stone was used in the coronation of Scottish kings. Its symbolic importance was so great that it was said, "Whoever holds the Stone of Scone holds Scotland."

Capture and Return

In 1296, during the conquest of Scotland by King Edward I of England, the stone was taken as war spoils and placed beneath the Coronation Chair in Westminster Abbey, London, where it was used in the coronations of English and later British monarchs. After centuries of dispute over its rightful ownership, the stone was finally returned to Scotland in 1996, on the condition that it would be loaned out for future coronations in the United Kingdom.

Mysteries and Legends

Some believe that the original stone was hidden by the monks of Scone, and a replica was handed over to Edward I. This theory suggests that the true Stone of Destiny is still somewhere in Scotland, waiting to be discovered. Other legends speak of its supposed biblical origin, suggesting the stone could be the same one Jacob used as a pillow when he dreamed of the ladder to heaven, making it an object of deep religious and mystical significance.

The Stone Today

From 1996 the Stone of Destiny rested in the Crown Room of Edinburgh Castle, where it was a popular attraction for visitors from around the world. Its return to Scotland was a moment of great national pride and symbolised the long and complex relationship between Scotland and England. The stone continues to be a powerful symbol of Scottish heritage and identity, shrouded in mystery and tradition. Since March 2024 the Stone has been on display at the new Perth Museum.

BRAVEHEART AND ROBERT THE BRUCE

The nickname "Braveheart" is often associated with William Wallace due to the popular film; however, it originally belonged to Robert the Bruce. This historical mix-up highlights the rich tapestry of Scottish history and its legendary figures.

Robert the Bruce, a national hero and King of Scots, played a crucial role in Scotland's fight for independence in the 14th century. The moniker "Braveheart" was attributed to him, symbolising his courage and leadership during the Wars of Scottish Independence.

The blending of these two historical figures in popular culture showcases the enduring fascination with Scotland's past and the legendary status of its heroes.

ANCIENT TREE

Scotland is home to a truly natural wonder: the oldest tree in Europe, a yew tree that is over 3,000 years old. This ancient yew, situated in the Scottish Highlands, stands as a living testament to the country's rich natural history. The tree has witnessed millennia of history, making it a symbol of resilience and continuity.

Despite its age, the tree remains in robust health, drawing visitors and nature enthusiasts from around the world. Its longevity offers a unique perspective on environmental stewardship and the importance of preserving natural heritage.

The ancient yew is not just a tree: it's a living piece of history, connecting the present day to a distant, almost mythical past. It serves as a reminder of the timeless beauty of Scotland's landscapes and the enduring power of nature.

UFO CAPITAL: BONNYBRIDGE

Bonnybridge, a small town in Scotland, has gained an unusual reputation as the UFO capital of the world. With over 300 reported sightings a year, it has become a hotspot for extraterrestrial enthusiasts and researchers.

This curious phenomenon has made Bonnybridge a subject of fascination and speculation. The high number of sightings has attracted global attention, sparking debates and discussions about the existence of extraterrestrial life. Whether these sightings are evidence of alien visitors or not, they have certainly put Bonnybridge on the map, adding an intriguing layer to Scotland's diverse and mysterious landscape.

VIKING TREASURE IN SHETLAND AND ORKNEY

The Shetland and Orkney islands, at the northernmost tip of Scotland, hold a rich legacy of the Vikings, evidenced by numerous treasures and archaeological sites. Dominated by the Norse from the late 8th century, these islands served as strategic centres for Viking exploration, trade, and raids. Among the most notable finds are intricate pieces of jewellery, weapons, and household items that reveal the Vikings' high level of skill and aesthetic.

One of the most emblematic sites is the Viking village of Jarlshof in Shetland which displays layers of history from prehistoric dwellings to ruins from the Viking period. In Orkney, the Maeshowe tomb offers a glimpse into Viking art and beliefs, with runes carved by Norse visitors that recount their exploits and thoughts.

These archaeological discoveries not only enrich our understanding of the Viking presence in Scotland but also highlight the importance of these islands as a vital link between Norse and Scottish cultures. The Viking legacy in Shetland and Orkney is a lasting testament to the cultural exchange and influence that shaped the history of these fascinating regions.

RIGHT OF WAY LAWS

Scotland stands out for its progressive approach to public access to private land, thanks to the Land Reform Act of 2003. This legislation allows people to walk, cycle, swim, and camp in almost all areas of the country, promoting respect for nature and property. Users are encouraged to follow the Scottish Outdoor Access Code, ensuring a balance between enjoying Scotland's landscapes and environmental preservation. The law supports a variety of outdoor activities and fosters a harmonious relationship between the population, the land, and its owners, reflecting Scotland's commitment to freedom of access and environmental responsibility.

CLACH AN TRUSHAL STONE

The Clach an Trushal Stone, located near the Harris Islands on the island of Lewis, is recognised as the tallest standing stone in Scotland, reaching about 6 metres in height. This prehistoric monument, possibly part of an ancient stone circle, is shrouded in mystery, reflecting the ritual or social practices of the Neolithic communities. Its exact origin and purpose remain an enigma, with theories ranging from astronomical functions to sites of spiritual significance. The Clach an Trushal Stone captures the imagination, serving as a silent testament to the ancient civilisations that once inhabited these islands.

THE CLAN CEMETERY IN INVERNESS

The Clan Cemetery, located near Inverness Castle, is an historic site where Scottish clan leaders are buried. This cemetery is a testament to the ancient rivalries and rich history of Scotland's clans. Serving as a tangible record of the complex social dynamics of the Highlands, the cemetery reflects the traditions, honours, and struggles faced by these powerful families throughout history. Visiting the Clan Cemetery offers a window into the tumultuous past and deep culture of the Scottish Highlands.

THE MYSTERY OF THE GLASGOW NECROPOLIS

In the heart of Glasgow, the Necropolis hides among its tombs a mystery that has lasted for generations: the legend of the Vanishing Mausoleum. It is said that in 1832, an entire mausoleum simply disappeared overnight, leaving no trace. Since then, reports of a hooded figure wandering where the mausoleum is supposed to be have fuelled speculation about eternal guardians and ancient secrets.

Research into historical records has revealed little and the mystery of the Vanishing Mausoleum remains, provoking the imagination of all who visit the Necropolis. Is it just an urban legend or is there a grain of truth in this enigmatic story? What we do know is that the Glasgow Necropolis is a place where stories and secrets intertwine, some of which may never be revealed.

PART II

NATURAL WONDERS

FAIRY POOLS AND THE NATURAL BEAUTY OF THE ISLE OF SKYE

The Isle of Skye, located off the west coast of Scotland, is renowned for its spectacular and mystical landscapes, and among its many natural treasures are the Fairy Pools: a series of crystal-clear natural pools and waterfalls located at the foot of the Black Cuillins. The water, so clear that one can see to the bottom, varies in shades of blue and green depending on the light and viewing angle, creating a magical setting.

The name "Fairy Pools" evokes images of Celtic legends and fairy tales that are a rich part of Scottish folklore. It is believed that these pools were sacred sites for the ancient Celts, who saw them as portals to the fairy world or places of spiritual power. Today, the Fairy Pools attract visitors from around the globe.

The hike to the Fairy Pools unveils the wild beauty of Skye, with its towering mountains, verdant valleys, and expansive skies. This location is not just a highlight of

Scotland's natural beauty but also a reminder of the deep connection between the land and the stories that shape Scottish cultural identity

ISLE OF IONA

The Isle of Iona, off the west coast of Scotland, is a small island with a big history. Known as the cradle of Scottish Christianity, it's where Saint Columba established a monastery in 563 AD. This monastery played a pivotal role in spreading Christianity throughout Scotland.

Iona Abbey, one of the oldest and most important religious centres in Western Europe, stands as a testament to the island's spiritual heritage. The abbey is a place of tranquility and reflection, attracting thousands of pilgrims and visitors each year.

The history of Iona is not just confined to its religious significance. It's also a place of breathtaking natural beauty, with pristine beaches and a serene landscape that has captivated visitors for centuries. The island's unique blend of spiritual and natural heritage makes it a gem in Scotland's crown.

THE 56TH PARALLEL NORTH

Scotland is geographically situated along the 56th parallel North, a location it shares with notable areas such as Denmark and parts of Canada. This geographical position contributes to Scotland's unique climate, its long summer nights and short winter days, a fundamental aspect of Scottish life.

Climate and light influence everything from cultural traditions to agriculture and the region's ecology. In Scotland, summer nights can be incredibly long, with twilights lasting until midnight, creating a magical atmosphere during the warmer months.

In winter, the opposite occurs, with short days that are offset by warm winter celebrations such as Hogmanay. This intimate relationship with nature and the seasons is a key element of Scottish culture and identity.

THE MYSTERIES OF THE OLD MAN OF STORR

The Old Man of Storr, with their towering silhouettes rising against the horizon of the Isle of Skye, are more than mere rock formations: they are the epicentre of mysteries and legends that have captivated and intrigued both locals and visitors for centuries. This singular place, shrouded in fog and mystery, serves as a gateway to Scotland's mythic past, where folklore and landscape intertwine inseparably.

The Legend of the Giant

One of the most evocative legends related to the Old Man of Storr is that of the petrified giant. It is said that these rocks are the remnants of an ancient giant who once dwelled in the land, his body turned to stone by magic or the wrath of the gods. The "Old Man" itself is purported to be the giant's thumb, eternally pointing towards the sky, a formidable reminder of his presence and power.

Another legendary interpretation sees the Old Man of Storr as ancestral guardians of the island. These formidable stone structures are considered eternal sentinels, watching over Skye and protecting it from malevolent forces. It is believed that, by walking among these "guardians," one can feel the energy and spirit of those who the island harboured in bygone eras.

Portals to Other Worlds

Many stories revolve around the Old Man of Storr as portals to other worlds or dimensions. According to local folklore, certain spots around these rocks serve as gateways to the realm of the fairies, a parallel world inhabited by mystical beings. These passages, invisible to the eyes of ordinary mortals, can only be revealed under special circumstances or to those chosen by the fairies.

Reports of supernatural encounters in the vicinity of the Old Man of Storr are common, with visitors recounting fleeting visions of ethereal figures or hearing unexplained sounds, such as music coming from nowhere. Such experiences reinforce the belief that this place is not just a natural wonder, but a space where the veil between the natural and the supernatural is particularly thin.

The fascination with the mysteries of the Old Man of Storr transcends the location itself, inspiring a rich tapestry of myths, legends, and artworks. Poets, writers, and artists have sought to capture the enigmatic essence of these rock formations, transforming them into symbols of mystery, beauty, and the eternal human quest for meaning amidst the vastness of nature.

The Old Man of Storr remain as one of Scotland's most mysterious and legendary treasures, a place where the stories of the past meet the spiritual quests of the present, and where mystery continues to envelop every stone and every whisper of the wind.

LOCH LOMOND & THE TROSSACHS

Loch Lomond & The Trossachs National Park is a natural jewel in Scotland's crown. Encompassing the largest lake in Great Britain by surface area, Loch Lomond, and the scenic Trossachs region offers a landscape of stunning beauty and diversity.

Loch Lomond, with its tranquil waters and picturesque islands, is a haven for boating, water sports, and wildlife-watching. The surrounding mountains, including Ben Lomond, provide challenging hikes and panoramic views of the Scottish countryside.

The Trossachs, often referred to as 'Scotland in miniature', is an area of wooded glens, braes, and lochs. It has inspired poets and artists for centuries with its enchanting scenery. This area is not just a destination for outdoor enthusiasts; it's a place where one can experience the tranquil beauty of Scottish nature at its best.

THE AURORA BOREALIS IN SCOTLAND

Scotland, with its location in the northern part of Great Britain, is one of the few places in the world where the spectacular light show of the aurora borealis can be witnessed. These dancing lights, known as "Mirrie Dancers" by the Scots, are a natural phenomenon caused by the interaction between the sun's charged particles and the Earth's magnetic field.

The best times to see the auroras in Scotland are during the winter months when the nights are longest and the sky is sufficiently dark. Places like Shetland, Orkney, and the

North Coast 500 offer unobstructed views of the night sky, transforming into stages for this spectacle of lights. Observing the aurora borealis is a transcendental experience, connecting viewers to the vastness of the universe and the beauty of Scotland's wild nature.

The phenomenon of the aurora borealis, beyond being a beautiful natural spectacle, carries with it myths and legends local to the culture. In Scottish culture, the "Mirrie Dancers" have been viewed throughout the centuries as messengers of future events, both fortunate and ominous. This connection between the sky and human fate reflects the deep reverence Scots have for the natural world and its power to inspire, awe, and sometimes intimidate.

FINGAL'S CAVE: THE BASALT ORGAN OF THE ATLANTIC

Enveloped in the swirling mists of the Scottish seas lies Fingal's Cave, a cavern of geometric marvels on the desolate Isle of Staffa. More than a mere natural wonder, it's a cathedral forged by the elements, its hexagonal basalt columns resembling the pipes of a giant organ. Legends whisper that these pillars were not solely the work of volcanic eruptions and the ocean's sculpting hands over millions of years, but also of giants from the mists of time, particularly the legendary giant Fingal, for whom the cave is named.

The cave's otherworldly acoustics, which lend the air an ethereal quality, inspired the composer Felix Mendelssohn to create the "Hebrides Overture," capturing the haunting beauty and the murmuring echoes of this ancient place. But beyond its musical inspiration, local lore speaks of the cave as a gateway to the Otherworld, a mystical realm in Celtic mythology where heroes and gods dwell. It's said that Fingal's Cave is part of a larger, supernatural causeway built by giants, connecting Scotland with Ireland's Giant's Causeway, a testament to the intertwined destinies of these lands and their colossal inhabitants.

Facing the relentless sea, Fingal's Cave stands as a sentinel at the boundary of our world and the mythic, its entrance a portal through which one might glimpse the ancient spirits and tales that have shaped the Celtic world. Visitors to the cave often speak of an overwhelming sense of the past that pervades the air, a feeling that the legends and myths might just have a foot in reality. In the echoes of the waves within the cave, some hear the voices of ancient heroes and the distant footsteps of giants, forever linking Fingal's Cave to the rich tapestry of Celtic legend and the timeless allure of Scotland's natural landscape.

THE MIRROR OF GLEN COE: THE LAKE OF DREAMS

Glen Coe, one of the most spectacular and dramatically beautiful landscapes in Scotland, harbours a lesser-known but equally fascinating natural phenomenon: the "Lake of Dreams." On calm mornings, when the waters of the lake settle, the surface of the lake transforms into a perfect mirror, reflecting the towering mountains, verdant valleys, and the blue sky above. This natural mirror not only doubles the already staggering beauty of Glen Coe but also creates a moment of pure magic, where sky and earth seem to merge. It is said that those who witness this spectacle carry with them a sense of peace and wonder that lasts a lifetime. The Lake of Dreams is a reminder of the ephemeral beauty and the immutable majesty of Scottish nature.

PART III

MANMADE WONDERS

GLENFINNAN VIADUCT

The Glenfinnan Viaduct in the Scottish Highlands is a spectacular example of Victorian engineering and design. Made famous by its appearance in the Harry Potter film series, the viaduct has become an iconic symbol of Scotland's rugged and picturesque landscape.

Constructed in the late 19th century, the viaduct's 21 towering arches majestically span across the Glenfinnan valley, offering breathtaking views of Loch Shiel and the surrounding mountains. This engineering marvel was built to extend the West Highland Railway line and is a testament to Scotland's industrial heritage.

The Glenfinnan Viaduct is not just a functional railway bridge: it's a destination for tourists and train enthusiasts. The Jacobite steam train, which passes over the viaduct, offers a journey back in time, showcasing the stunning natural beauty of the Scottish Highlands.

BELL ROCK LIGHTHOUSE

The Bell Rock Lighthouse, located off the coast of Angus, Scotland, is one of the seven industrial wonders of the world. Constructed between 1807 and 1810 by engineer Robert Stevenson, it stands as the world's oldest surviving sea-washed lighthouse. Built on a partially submerged reef, the lighthouse presented a formidable engineering challenge.

The success of Bell Rock Lighthouse marked a significant advancement in maritime safety, guiding ships away from the perilous Inchcape Rock. Its construction is a story of determination and innovation, embodying Scotland's rich history in engineering and maritime navigation.

THE SECRET GARDEN OF DUNROBIN

In the north of Scotland stands the majestic Dunrobin Castle, the ancestral home of the Clan Sutherland. With its pointed towers and a silhouette that evokes fairy tales, Dunrobin seems more a dream setting than a medieval stronghold. However, it is in its vast gardens that one of the castle's most enchanting secrets is revealed: a secret garden inspired by the extravagant French gardens of the Palace of Versailles.

This garden, hidden from public view and accessible only from the castle, is a testament to the luxury and attention to detail characteristic of Scottish nobility. With its perfect symmetry, dancing fountains, and variety of exotic flowers, Dunrobin's secret garden is an oasis of tranquility and beauty. It is said that on misty mornings, the garden takes on an ethereal air, as if it were a portal to an enchanted world, shielded from time and history.

The existence of this garden is a reminder of the Scots' passion for nature and landscape design, as well as a symbol of the intimate connection between architecture and the natural environment in Scotland. Visiting Dunrobin's secret garden offers a unique experience, providing a different perspective on the cultural and natural heritage of this country.

ROSSLYN CHAPEL AND ITS MYSTERIES

Rosslyn Chapel, located just outside Edinburgh, is shrouded in mystery and speculation. Built in the 15th century by the St. Clair family, the chapel is a treasure trove of Gothic art, famous for its intricate stone carvings that cover nearly every inch of its interior. However, it is the abundance of mystical symbols and alleged connections to the Knights Templar and the Holy Grail that have fuelled the imagination of historians, conspiracy theorists, and visitors for centuries.

The complexity of the carvings, which include depictions of biblical scenes, mythological figures, medicinal plants, and supposedly scenes from the New World before its "official" discovery by Christopher Columbus, suggest that the chapel served purposes beyond conventional religious and spiritual ones. Some theories propose that Rosslyn Chapel may have been a secret meeting place for the Templars, safeguarding sacred relics and hidden knowledge.

The aura of mystery has been amplified by modern fiction, most notably Dan Brown's "The Da Vinci Code," which placed Rosslyn Chapel at the heart of a global plot involving secret societies and hidden treasures. Regardless of the truth behind these stories, the chapel continues to be a fascinating point of study for those interested in medieval history, religious symbolism, and legends.

THE GLASGOW NECROPOLIS

One of Europe's most significant and atmospheric cemeteries, serves as a grand testament to Scotland's rich historical and architectural heritage. Perched on a scenic hill overlooking Glasgow, this vast cemetery, with more than 50,000 graves, is not just a final resting place but a reflection of the Victorian era's fascination with death and nature. Inspired by Père Lachaise in Paris and established in 1832, the Necropolis is a stunning example of funerary art, showcasing a range of monumental tombs, mausoleums, and sculptures that tell the stories of the people interred within, from influential Glaswegians to notable figures in Scottish history.

As visitors wander its winding paths, they are enveloped in a serene yet poignant atmosphere, where each monument reveals insights into the social, cultural, and economic fabric of the time. The Necropolis is a vivid portrayal of Victorian Glasgow's societal divisions, with the grandeur of monuments often reflecting the deceased's social status. It stands as a cultural beacon, offering a unique window into the attitudes towards death, the afterlife, and the importance of memorialisation in the 19th century.

Today, the Glasgow Necropolis attracts scholars, tourists, and locals alike, drawn to its tranquil beauty and historical significance. It serves as a powerful reminder of our mortality and the legacy we leave behind, making it a place of reflection and learning. The Necropolis is not just a cemetery; it's a celebration of life, death, and the enduring stories of those who came before us, ensuring that their memories continue to inspire and educate future generations.

GLASGOW GREEN AND THE DOULTON FOUNTAIN

Glasgow Green, the oldest public park in the city, stands as a verdant testament to Glasgow's rich history and commitment to public spaces. Amidst its expansive lawns and ancient trees lies a remarkable piece of Victorian-era craftsmanship: the Doulton Fountain, renowned as the largest terracotta fountain in the world. This magnificent fountain, gifted to the city by Sir Henry Doulton in 1888, was originally showcased at the International Exhibition before finding its permanent home in Glasgow Green. Its intricate design and detailed sculptures reflect the artistic and industrial prowess of the period, offering a glimpse into the Victorian fascination with ornamental beauty and technological advancement.

The Doulton Fountain is more than just an architectural marvel: it's a symbol of the city's Victorian heritage, representing the era's optimism and the burgeoning public park movement that sought to provide green spaces for relaxation and recreation to the urban populace. The fountain's elaborate structure, featuring a series of basins and statues representing different parts of the British Empire, speaks to the global ambitions and imperial connections of Britain during the Victorian age. Today, as visitors meander through Glasgow Green and encounter the majestic fountain, they are transported to a time when Glasgow was at the forefront of the Industrial Revolution, embodying the city's dynamic spirit and its role in shaping the modern world. The preservation of the Doulton Fountain, along with the continuous enjoyment and appreciation of Glasgow Green, ensures that these historic treasures continue to enrich the cultural landscape of Glasgow, serving as enduring reminders of the city's past and its ongoing legacy.

SCOTLAND'S STONEHENGE:

THE CALLANISH STONES

The Callanish Stones, often referred to as "Scotland's Stonehenge", are an impressive and mysterious prehistoric stone arrangement located on the Isle of Lewis. Estimated to have been erected around 3000 BC, these standing stones form a cruciform pattern with a central stone circle. Their purpose remains a subject of speculation, with theories ranging from astronomical alignments to religious ceremonies.

The Callanish Stones are a poignant reminder of Scotland's ancient past and the sophistication of its early inhabitants. The site attracts visitors from all over the world, drawn to its historical significance and the mystical atmosphere that surrounds it. The stones are not just a tourist attraction but a symbol of Scotland's rich archaeological heritage.

BALNAIN HOUSE

Balnain House, nestled in the heart of Inverness, is a building steeped in history and mystery. Known for its alleged paranormal activities, it attracts those intrigued by the supernatural. Originally serving as a residence for notable figures, Balnain House has since been transformed into a venue for music and arts, celebrating the cultural heritage of the Highlands. However, it's the tales of ghostly apparitions and unexplained phenomena that continue to capture the imagination of locals and visitors alike. Exploring Balnain House offers a unique blend of cultural enrichment and a peek into the spectral tales that weave through the fabric of Inverness's history.

GEORGE SQUARE IN GLASGOW

George Square, in the heart of Glasgow, is a hub of cultural and historical interest. Surrounded by architecturally significant buildings, including the Glasgow City Chambers, the square has been the focal point of the city since the 19th century.

The square hosts various statues and monuments, including those of famous Scots such as Robert Burns and Sir Walter Scott. It has been a venue for political rallies, celebrations, and public events, playing a key role in the civic life of Glasgow.

George Square is not just a public space: it's a living museum of Glasgow's history and a testament to the city's vibrant culture. It's a place where the past and present of Glasgow converge, making it a must-visit for anyone exploring the city.

MACKINTOSH AND THE GLASGOW SCHOOL OF ART

Charles Rennie Mackintosh, a renowned Scottish architect and designer, made a significant contribution to Glasgow's architectural heritage with his design of the Glasgow School of Art. This building is considered one of the finest examples of Art Nouveau in the world and showcases Mackintosh's innovative and distinctive style.

The Glasgow School of Art was not just a building: it was a manifestation of Mackintosh's vision of blending functionality with artistic flair. The school's unique design features include the use of natural motifs, distinctive geometric forms, and the harmonious blend of different materials.

Mackintosh's influence extends beyond the school, as he left a lasting legacy on Glasgow's architectural and cultural landscape. His work continues to inspire architects and designers worldwide, and the Glasgow School of Art remains a symbol of innovation and creativity in Scottish design.

PRINCES STREET GARDENS

Princes Street Gardens in Edinburgh is a picturesque public park nestled in the heart of the city. Lying in the shadow of Edinburgh Castle, these gardens provide a peaceful escape from the bustle of city life.

Originally the site of the Nor Loch, a medieval defensive barrier for the castle, the area was transformed into the beautiful gardens seen today. The gardens are split into two sections – the East and West gardens – each offering its own unique charm and historical monuments.

Princes Street Gardens is not just a green space: it's a cultural and historical hub. The gardens host various events and festivals throughout the year, including Christmas markets and New Year celebrations. The Ross Bandstand, an open-air venue in the gardens, is a focal point for live performances. Walking through the gardens, visitors can enjoy spectacular views of the castle and the city's skyline, making it a favourite spot for locals and tourists alike

ST ANDREWS

St. Andrews, known worldwide as the birthplace of golf, is a city full of history and charm. Located on the east coast of Scotland, it is home to the famous Old Course, one of the oldest and most prestigious golf courses in the world. But St. Andrews is more than just golf: it is also home to one of Scotland's oldest and most renowned universities.

The University of St. Andrews, founded in 1413, is an institution rich in academic tradition and historic architecture. The city, with its cobblestone streets and medieval buildings, is a dive into Scottish history. St. Andrews also offers stunning beaches and a vibrant cultural scene, making it a must-see destination in Scotland. Additionally, St. Andrews has significant religious importance, being the site of St. Andrews Cathedral, once the largest religious building in Scotland. Today, its ruins evoke a deep spiritual past and the city's importance in Scottish Christianity.

SCOTT MONUMENT

The Scott Monument in Edinburgh is a towering tribute to Sir Walter Scott, one of Scotland's most famous writers. Standing at over 200 feet tall, it's the largest monument to a writer anywhere in the world.

The monument's gothic design is adorned with statues and carvings depicting characters from Scott's novels, showcasing the impact of his work on Scottish literature. Visitors can climb the monument's narrow spiral staircase to enjoy panoramic views of Edinburgh.

The Scott Monument is not just a memorial: it's a testament to the enduring legacy of Sir Walter Scott's contributions to literature and to the cultural heritage of Scotland.

HARRIS TWEED

Harris is world-renowned for its Harris Tweed, a handcrafted woollen fabric that has legal protection for its authenticity. Harris Tweed is not only famous for its durability and quality, but also for its unique patterns that reflect the island's natural landscape. The weaving tradition is a vital part of the local economy and cultural heritage.

THE SCOTTISH DARK SKY OBSERVATORY: A GATEWAY TO THE COSMOS

Located near Dalmellington on the edge of the Galloway Forest Park, the Scottish Dark Sky Observatory offers a unique opportunity to gaze at the stars from one of the few "Dark Sky Parks" in Europe. This observatory is situated in an area with minimal light pollution, providing unparalleled views of the night sky, including planets, galaxies, and meteor showers.

The observatory is equipped with state-of-the-art telescopes and offers public and private viewing sessions, educational programmes, and special events designed to inspire and educate visitors about astronomy and the importance of preserving dark skies. It stands as a testament to Scotland's commitment to environmental conservation and its fascination with the mysteries of the universe.

Each of these unique events and locations offers a glimpse into the diverse cultural fabric of contemporary

Scotland, celebrating everything from its ancient traditions to its contributions to global culture and science.

PART IV

CULTURE, TRADITIONS, AND INNOVATIONS

Scotland is a land of profound contrasts, where rich cultural and historical heritage meets a legacy of innovation and discovery that has changed the world. In this part, we will explore the unique traditions and festivals that keep Scotland's cultural roots alive, as well as the innovations and contributions that have emanated from this land to reach across the globe.

SCOTLAND'S NATIONAL DAY

St. Andrew's Day, celebrated on the 30th of November, is Scotland's national day, commemorating Saint Andrew, the patron saint of Scotland. The day is marked with a celebration of Scottish culture, including traditional music, dance, food, and, of course, plenty of Scottish whisky.

The festivities often extend beyond Scotland's borders, celebrated by Scottish communities around the world. St. Andrew's Day is not just a day of national pride: it is also an opportunity to showcase Scotland's rich heritage and traditions, reinforcing the bonds that connect Scots no matter where they are in the world.

HOGMANAY: THE SCOTTISH NEW YEAR

Hogmanay is Scotland's celebration of the New Year and is undoubtedly one of the country's most spectacular and eagerly awaited festivities. Unlike any other New Year celebration in the world, Hogmanay blends ancient pagan rituals with traditions passed down through generations. From torchlit processions and bonfires lighting up the night to purify the coming year, to singing "Auld Lang Syne" hand-in-hand at midnight, Hogmanay is a powerful expression of Scottish culture.

One of the most distinctive elements of Hogmanay is "First Footing," a tradition stating that the first person to cross the threshold of a home after midnight will determine the household's fortune for the coming year. Traditionally, the ideal "first-footer" should be a tall, dark-haired man bringing gifts such as coal, whisky, or homemade bread, symbolising warmth, good luck, and prosperity.

THREE OFFICIAL LANGUAGES

Scotland officially recognises three languages: English, Scottish Gaelic, and Scots. This linguistic diversity reflects the country's rich cultural heritage and history.

Scottish Gaelic, a Celtic language, has its roots in the Highlands and is a vital part of Scottish identity. Scots, a Germanic language, is spoken in various regions and has contributed significantly to Scottish literature and everyday life.

The presence of these three languages demonstrates Scotland's commitment to preserving its linguistic heritage and promoting cultural diversity within its borders.

SCOTTISH INVENTIONS: TELEPHONE AND TELEVISION

Scotland's legacy of innovation is highlighted by two groundbreaking inventions: the telephone by Alexander Graham Bell and the first television picture by John Logie Baird. These inventions have had a profound impact on global communication and entertainment.

Bell, born in Edinburgh, invented the telephone in 1876, revolutionising the way people communicate. His invention laid the groundwork for the modern telecommunications industry, changing society forever.

John Logie Baird, another Scottish inventor, displayed the first television picture in the 1920s. His work paved the way for one of the most influential mediums in entertainment and news broadcasting. Baird's television became a pivotal invention, transforming media consumption and communication, and marking Scotland's place in the history of technological innovation.

PENICILLIN: A PIONEERING SCOTTISH CONTRIBUTION TO MODERN MEDICINE

The discovery of penicillin by Scottish bacteriologist Alexander Fleming in 1928 marked a significant milestone in the field of medicine. This breakthrough occurred in a London laboratory, where Fleming noticed that the Penicillium notatum mould could kill bacteria. This led to the development of the first widely-used antibiotic, revolutionising the treatment of bacterial infections and saving countless lives.

Before penicillin, infections like pneumonia and syphilis were often fatal. The introduction of this antibiotic during the 1940s significantly lowered mortality rates from such diseases. Its development into a drug suitable for mass production, thanks to the efforts of scientists like Howard Florey. Ernst Boris Chain was critical in making it accessible worldwide especially during World War II.

The advent of penicillin not only transformed medical practice by providing an effective treatment for various infections but also laid the groundwork for the development of other antibiotics. Fleming, Florey, and Chain's work earned them the Nobel Prize in Physiology or Medicine in 1945, highlighting the global impact of this Scottish discovery on modern medicine.

THE ART OF DISTILLATION: SCOTCH WHISKY

Scotch whisky is celebrated worldwide for its quality and tradition. The art of whisky distillation in Scotland dates back centuries and is an intrinsic part of the national identity. Each region of Scotland produces its own distinct type of whisky, from the rich and peaty malts of Islay to the smooth and floral ones of Speyside. The production of whisky is both a science and an art, involving knowledge passed down through generations, from selecting the grain to the lengthy aging in wooden barrels. This gives Scotch whisky its unique and complex flavour.

SCOTTISH HERITAGE IN THE USA

The influence of Scottish heritage in the United States is significant, with more people of Scottish descent living in the U.S. than in Scotland itself. This is a result of centuries of migration, contributing to the cultural and historical ties between the two nations. Scottish immigrants have played a vital role in shaping American society, politics, and culture. Their contributions are evident in various aspects of American life, from the Declaration of Independence to innovations in industry and science.

The strong Scottish presence in the USA is a reminder of the far-reaching impact of Scotland's people and culture, extending well beyond its geographical borders.

THE BELTANE FIRE FESTIVAL: A MODERN REVIVAL OF ANCIENT CELTIC TRADITIONS

The Beltane Fire Festival stands as a vibrant testament to Scotland's ability to blend ancient customs with contemporary celebration. Held annually on the 30th of April on Calton Hill in Edinburgh, this festival marks the beginning of the summer season, reviving the ancient Celtic tradition of celebrating the power of the sun, fertility, and the renewal of life. The Beltane Fire Festival is not just an event: it's a spectacle of fire, drumming, costume, and performance that draws thousands of spectators from around the globe.

Originating from the Gaelic May Day festival, Beltane was one of the four major Celtic seasonal festivals, alongside Samhain, Imbolc, and Lughnasadh. Traditionally, Beltane was the time when cattle were driven to summer pastures, and rituals were performed to protect them and encourage growth. Fires, symbolic of the sun, played a crucial role in the celebrations, believed to have protective powers.

The modern festival was reborn in 1988 as part of a movement to bring ancient Celtic traditions back to life in a contemporary context. Participants in the festival paint their faces and bodies, don elaborate costumes, and perform a series of rituals that culminate in the lighting of a massive bonfire. Central to the festival is the May Queen and the Green Man, symbolic figures who lead the procession and represent the fertility and growth that Beltane traditionally celebrates.

The Beltane Fire Festival is a unique cultural event that not only honours Scotland's pagan past but also embodies the spirit of community and creativity. It serves as a reminder of humanity's connection to the natural cycles of the earth, celebrated through a spectacle of fire and performance under the spring sky.

INVENTION OF THE WATERPROOF COAT

Scotland's contribution to practical attire includes the invention of the waterproof coat by Charles Macintosh. This innovation, dating back to the early 19th century, was a significant advancement in clothing technology, especially in a country known for its rainy weather.

Macintosh's process involved using rubber to waterproof fabric, a method that revolutionised the way people protected themselves from the elements. The 'Mac', as it came to be known, quickly became an essential item for outdoor wear, synonymous with practicality and durability.

The invention of the waterproof coat is a testament to Scottish ingenuity and adaptability, reflecting the nation's ability to create solutions suited to its unique climate and conditions.

THE UP HELLY AA FIRE FESTIVAL: A TRIBUTE TO VIKING HERITAGE

U p Helly Aa is a fire festival held in Lerwick, Shetland, on the last Tuesday of January each year, celebrating the islands' Viking heritage. This remarkable festival, which is arguably one of the most spectacular in Scotland, involves a series of marches and visitations, culminating in a torch-lit procession and the burning of a Viking galley.

This tradition, which began in the 1880s, serves as a means for the Shetland community to mark the end of the Yule season and pay homage to their Norse ancestors. The festival is led by the 'Guizer Jarl,' the chief guizer who, along with his squad, dresses in full Viking attire. After a day of visits and celebrations, the guizers march through the town, their torches creating a river of fire that lights up the night, leading to the dramatic burning of the Viking longship.

Up Helly Aa is more than just a fire festival: it's a testament to the strength and pride of the Shetland community and its deep-rooted connection to Norse tradition and history. It's a vivid reminder of Scotland's diverse cultural heritage and its capacity to celebrate history with fervour and spectacle.

THE WORLD PORRIDGE MAKING CHAMPIONSHIP: CELEBRATING SCOTLAND'S NATIONAL DISH

Porridge is a staple of Scottish cuisine, known for its simplicity, health benefits, and versatility. The World Porridge Making Championship, held annually in the small village of Carrbridge in the Cairngorms National Park, elevates this humble dish to a competitive art form. Since its inception in 1994, the championship has attracted chefs and porridge enthusiasts from around the world, all vying for the coveted title of "World Porridge Making Champion" and the "Golden Spurtle" trophy.

The competition is centred around the traditional Scottish porridge, made only with oats, water, and salt. However, there is also a "Speciality" category that allows for creative interpretations of porridge, incorporating various ingredients and flavours. The championship celebrates the simplicity and complexity of porridge, emphasising the skill required to perfect its texture and taste.

THE FIRST NEW YEAR'S FIRE FESTIVAL

In Scotland, the tradition of celebrating the New Year, or Hogmanay, with fire dates back to ancient times, connecting modern Scots to their pagan and Celtic roots. These fire celebrations, including torches, bonfires, and fireworks, are more than visual spectacles: they symbolise purification and renewal which are deeply-rooted concepts in Celtic beliefs. The ancient Celts celebrated the Winter Solstice with great bonfires to encourage the sun to return, banishing winter's darkness. Hogmanay, with its roots in this tradition, is not just a testament to cultural endurance but also reflects the ways nature and the cosmos were revered by ancient Scots.

THE TRUE ORIGIN OF HALLOWEEN

Modern Halloween can trace its origins back to the ancient Celtic festival of Samhain, marking the end of the harvest season and the beginning of winter. In Scotland, this night was a window to the other world when the veils between the living and the dead thinned, allowing spirits and fairies to cross over. The lanterns carved from turnips, a precursor to the jack-o'-lanterns, were meant to protect homes from malevolent spirits. These nocturnal practices, blending fear, respect for the supernatural, and the celebration of seasonality, are the backbone of modern Halloween, showing how a deeply Scottish festival transformed into a global phenomenon.

THE SECRET CODE OF SCOTTISH CLANS

Scottish tartans are recognised worldwide, but few know the complexity and hidden meaning behind these patterns. Each tartan is a time capsule, representing the history, alliances, and feuds of a clan. During the ban on tartans after the Jacobite Rebellion of 1745, these patterns became even more significant, acting as a silent symbol of resistance and Scottish identity. Additionally, specific tartan patterns could indicate social standing within the clan or serve as a form of coded communication during periods of conflict or prohibition.

PART V

RANDOM CURIOSITIES

HOME OF GOLF

Golf, one of the most popular sports worldwide, was invented in Scotland in the 15th century. The game has deep roots in Scottish history, with the Old Course at St. Andrews, known as the "Home of Golf," being a pilgrimage site for golf enthusiasts.

Scottish golf courses are renowned for their beauty and challenging nature, embodying the sport's tradition and the country's natural landscapes. Golf has been an integral part of Scottish culture for centuries, shaping local economies and international sports culture.

The creation of golf in Scotland and its enduring popularity worldwide highlights the country's contribution to global sports and its cultural significance.

WORLD'S SHORTEST COMMERCIAL FLIGHT

Scotland boasts the world's shortest commercial flight, a journey that takes a mere 47 seconds from Westray to Papa Westray in Orkney. This flight, operated by Loganair, covers a distance of only 1.7 miles (2.7 km), making it a unique feature in global aviation.

The flight serves as a vital link between the islands, highlighting the importance of connectivity in remote areas. Although short, the flight is a lifeline for residents, providing essential services and transport.

The record-setting flight is not just a curiosity: it symbolises the adaptability and resourcefulness of Scottish island communities in bridging distances and overcoming geographical challenges.

UNICORN AS A NATIONAL SYMBOL

The unicorn, chosen as the national symbol of Scotland, represents a fascinating element of Scottish culture. This mythological animal, a symbol of purity and strength, has been associated with Scotland since the 12th century. The presence of the unicorn in national coats of arms and symbols reflects the country's rich mythological tradition. Often depicted in chains, which symbolises the power of the king or queen over something so majestic, the unicorn extolls values such as purity, innocence and the sovereignty of the nation. Its image adorns many official places, coins and is even celebrated at cultural events, showing its continued importance in Scottish national identity.

BAN OF HAGGIS IN THE USA

Since the 1970s, the importation of haggis into the United States has been banned, primarily due to its traditional recipe that includes sheep's lung. Haggis, Scotland's national dish, is a savoury pudding containing sheep's heart, liver, and lungs, mixed with onions, oatmeal, suet, and spices.

The ban reflects differing food safety regulations between the two countries. However, it also highlights the cultural significance of haggis to Scottish heritage and cuisine. This dish, often enjoyed during Burns Night celebrations, remains a symbol of Scottish culinary tradition.

The ban on haggis has spurred interest and curiosity about the dish globally, making it an iconic representation of Scottish culture and gastronomy.

SCOTTISH BREAKFAST

A traditional Scottish breakfast is a hearty and fulfilling meal, designed to provide a strong start to the day. It typically includes black pudding, Lorne sausage, bacon, eggs, baked beans, mushrooms, tomatoes, and tattie scones, along with a strong pot of tea

This breakfast is a showcase of Scotland's love for robust flavours and substantial meals. Each element of the breakfast represents a part of Scotland's culinary traditions, from the savoury Lorne sausage to the uniquely Scottish black pudding. A traditional Scottish breakfast is not just a meal: it's a culinary experience that reflects the country's gastronomic history.

ORIGIN OF CHICKEN TIKKA MASALA

Chicken Tikka Masala, a dish beloved worldwide, is said to have been invented by a Pakistani chef in Glasgow in 1971. This culinary creation exemplifies the fusion of South Asian and British cuisines, symbolising Scotland's multicultural society.

The story goes that the chef, responding to a customer's request for a sauce with his chicken tikka, improvised with yogurt, cream, and spices, thus creating this now-iconic dish. Chicken Tikka Masala has since become a staple in British and global cuisine, often regarded as the UK's national dish.

This dish's creation in Glasgow is a testament to the city's diverse culinary landscape and its role in shaping modern British cuisine.

HIGHEST PROPORTION OF REDHEADS

Scotland boasts the highest proportion of redheads in the world, with approximately 13% of the population having naturally red hair. This distinctive trait is a point of pride and a recognisable symbol of Scottish identity.

The genetic prevalence of red hair in Scotland is not just a matter of appearance: it's a unique aspect of the nation's genetic makeup. This characteristic sets Scotland apart, adding to the country's diverse and vibrant cultural tapestry.

The abundance of redheads in Scotland is a subject of fascination and often celebrated in Scottish culture and folklore. It's a distinctive feature that adds to the rich diversity of the Scottish people and their heritage.

THE STONE SKIMMING CHAMPIONSHIPS

Every year, the small Isle of Easdale, off the west coast of Scotland, becomes the centre of an unusual but fiercely competitive event: The World Stone Skimming Championships. This quirky competition, which began in 1983, attracts participants from all corners of the world, each aiming to become the champion stone skimmer.

The rules are simple: competitors must skim a stone, which must bounce on the water at least three times, across the surface of an old slate quarry filled with water. The stones must be natural, unaltered, and fit within a specified size. The winner is the one whose stone travels the furthest.

What makes this championship particularly Scottish is not just the unique blend of skill, physics, and fun but also its location. Easdale was once the centre of a thriving slate quarrying industry, and the flooded quarries now serve as the perfect arenas for stone skimming. This event highlights the Scottish penchant for creating joyful community gatherings out of historical and natural landscapes.

LOCH NESS MONSTER

The Loch Ness Monster, affectionately known as "Nessie", is a legendary creature said to inhabit Loch Ness in the Scottish Highlands. The first recorded sighting dates back to 565 AD, and since then, Nessie has become a symbol of Scottish folklore and mystery.

The allure of the Loch Ness Monster has captivated the world, drawing tourists and enthusiasts hoping to catch a glimpse of this elusive creature. Nessie's legend has played a significant role in Scottish tourism, making Loch Ness one of Scotland's most famous landmarks.

Whether fact or fiction, the story of the Loch Ness Monster is a fascinating part of Scotland's cultural narrative, blending history, myth, and the allure of the unknown.

FIRST COLOUR PHOTOGRAPH

The first colour photograph in the world was taken in Scotland, marking a significant milestone in the history of photography. This groundbreaking achievement was made by the Scottish physicist James Clerk Maxwell in 1861. The photograph, of a tartan ribbon, was presented at a lecture by Maxwell in London and demonstrated the three-colour method, laying the foundation for modern colour photography.

This innovation was not just a technical achievement but also a moment that changed the way we capture and perceive the world. The ability to photograph in colour opened up new possibilities in artistic expression and documentation. Today, the legacy of Maxwell's work is evident in every colour image we see, a testament to Scotland's contributions to the world of science and art.

ORIGIN OF BAGPIPES

Contrary to popular belief, bagpipes were not invented in Scotland but have their origins in ancient Egypt. The instrument made its way to Scotland around the 15th century, where it became deeply integrated into Scottish culture. In Scotland, the bagpipes underwent significant modifications to become the Great Highland Bagpipe, known for its unique sound and association with Scottish tradition.

The transformation of the bagpipes in Scotland is reflective of the country's ability to adopt and adapt cultural elements, making them distinctly Scottish. Today, the bagpipes are a symbol of Scottish national pride and are played at various cultural events, military ceremonies, and in pipe bands around the world.

SHERLOCK HOLMES: A SCOTTISH CREATION

Sherlock Holmes, the world's most famous detective, was the creation of Scottish author Sir Arthur Conan Doyle. First appearing in print in 1887, Holmes is renowned for his keen observation, logical reasoning, and the use of forensic science to solve complex cases. Conan Doyle's creation has become an integral part of literary history and has been adapted into numerous films, television series, and stage productions.

The character of Sherlock Holmes, though based in London, carries the influence of Conan Doyle's Scottish upbringing, particularly in his methodical approach and shrewd intellect. Holmes' enduring popularity is a testament to Conan Doyle's storytelling prowess and his contribution to the mystery and detective genre.

HAGGIS: SCOTLAND'S NATIONAL DISH

Haggis, Scotland's national dish, is a savoury pudding containing sheep's pluck (heart, liver, and lungs), minced with onion, oatmeal, suet, spices, and salt, traditionally encased in the animal's stomach. This dish, often associated with the celebration of Burns Night, is deeply rooted in Scottish culture.

The origins of haggis are a matter of debate, but it is a prime example of traditional Scottish resourcefulness in cooking, utilising all parts of the animal. Despite its unusual ingredients, haggis has a rich, nutty, and savoury flavour, and it is commonly served with "neeps and tatties" (turnips and potatoes).

In the modern culinary scene, haggis has been adapted into various contemporary dishes, reflecting the versatility of this traditional Scottish fare. Its unique taste and cultural significance make haggis an enduring symbol of Scottish cuisine.

SCOTTISH CUISINE

Scottish cuisine is a rich tapestry of flavours and traditions, with dishes like Cullen Skink and Cranachan showcasing Scotland's culinary heritage. Cullen Skink, originating from the town of Cullen in Moray, is a hearty soup made from smoked haddock, potatoes, and onions, symbolising Scotland's connection to the sea and its love for comforting, homely dishes.

Cranachan, on the other hand, is a dessert that combines raspberries, cream, honey, whisky, and toasted oats, reflecting the natural bounty of Scotland's fields and farms. This dish is traditionally served at celebrations and is a testament to the simple yet rich flavours that Scottish cuisine is known for.

Scottish cuisine goes beyond haggis and whisky; it's a celebration of local produce and traditional cooking methods. From the Highlands to the coastal towns, each region adds its unique twist to the Scottish culinary landscape, making it a diverse and delightful gastronomic journey.

GLASGOW'S FUNERAL CARRIAGES

Glasgow is home to one of the last remaining funeral carriage factories in the world. This unique aspect of the city's industrial heritage highlights a time when funeral processions were elaborate affairs. The craftsmanship involved in creating these carriages is a blend of art and engineering, reflecting the solemn beauty and dignity of traditional Scottish funerals.

The funeral carriages of Glasgow are not just vehicles: they are works of art, adorned with intricate details and made with the utmost care. These carriages, drawn by horses, were a common sight in Victorian Glasgow, embodying the city's respect for the ritual of mourning.

Preserving this tradition, the factory continues to produce these carriages, serving as a living museum and a testament to Glasgow's rich history. It provides a fascinating glimpse into a bygone era and the city's commitment to preserving its cultural heritage.

SKYE TERRIER DOGS

The Skye Terrier is a breed of dog that originated in Scotland, specifically on the Isle of Skye. Known for their distinctive long coats, pointy ears, and loyal nature, Skye Terriers are a symbol of Scottish tenacity and spirit.

These small but sturdy dogs were originally bred to hunt and guard, and their courageous temperament is well-documented in Scottish folklore. Perhaps the most famous Skye Terrier was Greyfriars Bobby, who became known for his loyalty to his master, staying by his grave for 14 years.

Skye Terriers are more than just pets: they are a living part of Scotland's cultural history. While not as common today, they continue to be cherished for their unique appearance and loyal companionship, embodying the rugged and resilient character of the Scottish landscape from which they hail.

THE EDINBURGH FRINGE FESTIVAL

The Edinburgh Fringe Festival, held every August, is the largest arts festival in the world. Originating in 1947, it has grown into a global phenomenon, showcasing a diverse range of performances from international and local artists.

The festival is unique in its open-access philosophy, meaning anyone can perform, leading to an eclectic mix of shows ranging from theatre and comedy to music and dance. The Fringe transforms Edinburgh into a vibrant, dynamic hub of artistic expression, with performances taking place in theatres, pubs, and even on the streets.

The Edinburgh Fringe Festival is more than an event: it's a celebration of creativity and artistic freedom. It provides a platform for emerging artists to showcase their work and for audiences to experience an unparalleled variety of performances, playing a vital role in Scotland's cultural life.

SCOTCH PIE

The Scotch Pie, a staple of Scottish cuisine, is a small, double-crust meat pie filled traditionally with mutton or minced meat. Its origins can be traced back to the medieval period, and it has remained a popular dish throughout Scotland's history.

Known for its compact size and robust flavour, the Scotch Pie is a favourite at football matches and local bakeries. The pie's thick pastry shell is designed to be eaten by hand, making it a convenient and satisfying meal for workers and travellers.

The Scotch Pie is more than just a food item: it's a symbol of Scotland's culinary traditions. Its enduring popularity reflects the Scottish people's appreciation for hearty, simple fare that has stood the test of time.

THE ROYAL EDINBURGH MILITARY TATTOO

The Royal Edinburgh Military Tattoo is one of Scotland's most spectacular and revered events. Held annually on the Esplanade of Edinburgh Castle, the Tattoo is a dazzling display of military music, dance and displays of precision.

With participants from armies around the world, the event celebrates music, culture and military heritage in a stunning historical setting. The combination of bagpipe bands, military bands, cultural display teams and a grand fireworks display creates an unforgettable experience.

The Tattoo is not just an event for lovers of music and military tradition: it is a celebration of international unity and brotherhood. Year after year, the event attracts spectators from all over the world, establishing itself as one of the highlights of the Scottish cultural calendar.

EILEAN DONAN CASTLE

One of the most intriguing stories associated with Eilean Donan Castle is the legend of the Spanish warrior. During the first decades of the 18th century, amid the Jacobite risings seeking to restore the Stuarts to the British throne, a detachment of Spanish soldiers is said to have arrived at the castle to support the Jacobite cause. According to legend, one of these soldiers fell in love with a local girl, but met a tragic and premature end. They say that his spirit still roams the castle and the surrounding area, eternally waiting for a reunion with his beloved. Visitors and staff report seeing apparitions and hearing footsteps and whispers in the castle's rooms and corridors, especially at night.

Eilean Donan Castle, with its imposing silhouette reflected in the tranquil waters around it, is not only a monument to the art of Scottish medieval architecture, but also a keeper of secrets and legends that await to be discovered by those who are drawn to its enigmatic beauty and his mysterious past.

CONCLUSION

As we close our journey through the curiosities and mysteries of Scotland, we reflect on the rich and multifaceted tapestry this country presents. From ancient magic and deep-rooted traditions to modern innovations and paranormal phenomena, Scotland continues to fascinate and inspire both those who dwell on its soil and those who visit from distant lands. This book sought not only to shed light on lesser-known aspects of Scottish culture but also to celebrate the depth and diversity that make Scotland a truly unique place in the world.

Throughout the pages of this book, we hope to have sparked a deeper appreciation for Scotland's mysteries and beauty, encouraging readers to explore the stories and landscapes of this remarkable country for themselves. Our mission is to take these mysteries and curiosities to people around the world, sharing Scotland's enchanting tales and rich heritage far beyond its borders. And this is just the beginning: we look forward to bringing you much more in the upcoming editions. May Scotland's eternal allure continue to draw curious hearts and minds, perpetuating admiration for its traditions, history, and indomitable spirit. Join us as we continue to uncover and celebrate the untold stories and hidden gems of Scotland, ensuring that the legacy and allure of this captivating country reach every corner of the globe.

APPENDIX

GLOSSARY OF SCOTTISH TERMS

- **Hogmanay**: *The Scottish New Year.*
- **Ceilidh**: *A traditional Scottish social gathering involving folk dancing and music.*
- **Loch**: *A lake or a sea inlet in Scotland.*
- **Munro**: *A mountain in Scotland over 3,000 feet (914.4 m) high.*
- **Tartan**: *A patterned cloth associated with specific Scottish clans.*
- **Burns Night**: *An annual celebration in honor of Scottish poet Robert Burns on 25 January.*
- **Clans**: *Traditional family groups in Scotland, each with its own tartan and heraldry.*

THANK YOU FOR VENTURING INTO THE MYSTERIES!

Thank You for Unveiling the Mysteries!

As our journey through Scotland's natural and manmade wonders concludes, we're deeply thankful for your companionship in uncovering these hidden gems. Your curiosity and passion have been the cornerstone of this adventure.

We hope this book has kindled a deeper appreciation for Scotland's marvels in your heart and inspired you to explore further. If it has enriched your understanding or ignited your imagination, our mission is accomplished.

Your feedback is invaluable. A review on Amazon would greatly support our mission, allowing more explorers to join us in this discovery.

Thank you for being an integral part of this journey into the mysteries of the natural world.

Thank you for reading.

Lincoln Alencar

ACKNOWLEDGEMENTS

This book is the result of the passion and dedication of many individuals. I wish to express my profound gratitude to all who contributed to its realisation, from the initial sketches to the final work. To the historians, folklorists, and Scots who generously shared their stories and knowledge, my heartfelt thanks. To my readers, I hope this book has offered a window into the soul of Scotland and awakened a desire to discover even more about this extraordinary country.

This outline serves as a guide for readers and enthusiasts seeking to immerse themselves in the rich culture, traditions, and mysteries of Scotland, providing a starting point for future adventures in the land of lochs, castles, and eternal legends.

Printed in Great Britain
by Amazon